GREAT PITCHERS OF THE NEGRO LEAGUES

By Paul Hoblin

Content Consultant
Raymond Doswell, Ed.D.
Curator, Negro Leagues Baseball Museum

Published by ABDO Publishing Company, PO Box 398166, Minneapolis, MN 55439.
Copyright © 2013 by Abdo Consulting Group, Inc. International copyrights reserved
in all countries. No part of this book may be reproduced in any form without written
permission from the publisher. SportsZone™ is a trademark and logo of ABDO
Publishing Company.

Printed in the United States of America,
North Mankato, Minnesota
052012
902012

 THIS BOOK CONTAINS AT LEAST 10% RECYCLED MATERIALS.

Editor: Chrös McDougall
Series Designer: Emily Love

Photo Credits

Matty Zimmerman/AP Images, cover; Negro Leagues Baseball Museum, 7, 25, 33, 37,
41, 53; Mark Rucker/Transcendental Graphics, Getty Images, 9, 23, 28, 31, 48; Chicago
History Museum/Getty Images, 11; The Journal Gazette, Dean Musser Jr./AP Images,
14; Diamond Images/Getty Images, 16; National Baseball Hall of Fame Library/AP
Images, 21; X, 34; Bettmann/Corbis/AP Images, 45; George Strock/Time Life Pictures/
Getty Images, 50; AP Images, 56; Orlin Wagner/AP Images, 54

Design elements: Patricia Hofmeester/Shutterstock Images; Bryan Solomon/
Shutterstock Images

Library of Congress Cataloging-in-Publication Data
Hoblin, Paul.
  Great pitchers of the Negro Leagues / Paul Hoblin.
     p. cm. -- (The Negro baseball leagues)
  Includes bibliographical references.
  ISBN 978-1-61783-508-7
 1. Pitchers (Baseball) Biography--United States--Juvenile literature. 2. African
American baseball players--Biography--Juvenile literature. 3. Negro leagues--History--
Juvenile literature. 4. Baseball--United States--History--Juvenile literature. I. Title.
  GV865.A1H545 2013
  796.3570922--dc23
  [B]
                        2012005980

TABLE OF CONTENTS

INTRODUCTION

Baseball has been called America's pastime. Yet the professional sport has not always been open to everyone. Many of the game's most revered players—from sluggers Babe Ruth and Ty Cobb to pitchers Christy Mathewson and Walter Johnson—played during an era when black players were unofficially barred from Major League Baseball (MLB). So, with little other choice, the black players created their own leagues—the Negro Leagues.

Blacks began playing baseball during the mid-1800s, not long after the sport was founded. But from the beginning, they faced discrimination. In fact, many of the early all-black games were between teams made up of slaves. Black players did make inroads into organized baseball later in the century. Some even made it into the major leagues. But by 1900, an unofficial color line was drawn, preventing black players from playing on the biggest stage.

The Negro National League (NNL) was founded in 1920 as the first successfully organized Negro League. Other Negro Leagues later formed in the eastern and southern

United States. And some teams, not in any leagues, simply traveled the country performing in exhibition games.

Life could be very hard for the Negro Leagues teams. Blacks did not have the same rights as whites at the time. Hotels sometimes refused to house them. Restaurants refused to serve them. Pay was low compared to that of the major leaguers. Discrimination was just a fact of life.

Although the Negro Leagues were largely unknown to whites, the black community viewed them as success stories. The big games attracted a who's who of black society. And today, the greatest Negro Leagues players are rightfully recognized in the National Baseball Hall of Fame.

The Negro Leagues were at their height in the early 1940s, when many of the top white players were away fighting in World War II. MLB's color line was finally shattered in 1947, when Jackie Robinson played his first game for the Brooklyn Dodgers. Full integration soon followed, and the Negro Leagues faded away by the 1960s. But the exciting stories of legendary players of the Negro Leagues live on, reminding most of the world what it had missed out on during the early 1900s.

ANDREW "RUBE" FOSTER

Perhaps nobody had as strong an influence on the Negro Leagues as Andrew "Rube" Foster. As the famous Negro Leagues player and manager John "Buck" O'Neil once said, "Rube Foster *was* black baseball."

During his almost 30-year career, Foster was a pitcher, a scout, a manager, and a team owner. His most important role, however, was as the founder and commissioner of black baseball's first successful national league.

YOUNG PHENOM TO OLD ACE

Foster grew up in Texas during the late 1800s. By the time he was in eighth grade, he decided to leave both school and home to start a career in baseball.

Andrew "Rube" Foster

Foster toured the southern United States with the Waco Yellow Jackets. The all-black team played ball during the day and then tried to find places to sleep at night. It was not always easy, though. White communities often closed their doors to the Yellow Jackets. They would not let the black players stay in their hotels or eat in their restaurants. Some black communities shut out the Yellow Jackets, too. Black baseball players would later be a source of pride for many black Americans. During the early 1900s, however, many believed baseball players were undignified.

7

THE BUNT-AND-STEAL

Andrew "Rube" Foster might well have been the first person to employ the hit-and-run play. He had the hitter bunt, and he called the play a bunt-and-steal. Foster valued the play so much that he would not allow someone to play on his team unless he knew how to lay down a good bunt. To test a player's skill, Foster would set an upside-down hat in front of the plate. Then he would tell the player to bunt the ball into it. Before games, he had groundskeepers pack the baselines with mud and leave the infield grass as long as possible. Those strategies were intended to slow a bunt down and keep it fair.

This belief would change rapidly within black communities. Rube Foster was one of the main reasons for this change.

One way Foster impressed baseball fans was with his physical appearance. He stood 6 feet 4 inches tall and weighed well over 200 pounds. His body was shaped something like a barrel. Most of it was muscle. And Foster used his size to overpower batters with a sizzling fastball.

In 1901 Frank C. Leland was forming a new black team called the Chicago Union Giants. He wanted the young Foster on his roster. However, Leland first needed to make sure Foster could handle the competition. Leland warned Foster in a letter

Rube Foster, *back row and third from left in baseball uniform,* **pitched for this all-black all-star team in 1906.**

that the Giants planned to play the best white clubs around. "I fear nobody," Foster wrote back.

Foster proved up to the challenge in his first game with the Giants. He pitched a shutout.

Foster joined the Cuban X Giants in 1903. Until this time, he had relied only on his fastball. He could simply fire pitches past his opponents. Foster assumed he would be able to

9

continue to do so against any batter he faced with the Giants. That was not the case.

Pitchers usually shorten their windups when runners are on base. This makes it so the runners have less time to steal. But Foster did not bother shortening his windups when he began playing with the Giants. As a result, he would get into his windup and the base runners would steal the next base with ease.

Foster was able to overcome his struggles. Once he was willing to set aside his pride, he studied the game and its strategies more closely. Soon Foster was back to being a dominant pitcher. In fact, many eventually considered Foster to be one of the best pitchers of his era, black or white.

There were no established Negro Leagues in 1903. However, Foster's Cuban X Giants met the Philadelphia Giants to unofficially determine the champions of black baseball. Foster took the mound for four of his team's five wins. The Cuban X Giants won the series.

Foster shined against black opponents. He also gained some attention around this time for pitching to top white players. An unofficial color line barred blacks from playing in MLB. However, black teams would sometimes play white teams in exhibition games. In one, Foster pitched to MLB stars Mike Dolan and Jake Stahl. In both cases, the hitters could do

Rube Foster played for the Leland Giants in 1909.

nothing more than whiff. According to legend, Dolan struck out three times in a row. Stahl "couldn't get within speaking distance of . . . Rube's curves."

Foster was very strong. But for the rest of his pitching career, he used his brains as much as his physical abilities on the mound. Doing so allowed him to be effective even after his arm grew tired. Sometimes, he used mind games and even trickery to help get batters out.

Once, Foster was facing the great white hitter Topsy Hartsel. Foster called his catcher, James Booker, to the mound. He instructed Booker not to crouch behind the plate as he usually did. Instead, Booker was to stand up and off to the side of the plate. That is the standard way to announce an intentional walk.

By doing that, Hartsel would assume he did not need to pay attention. After all, he was going to be given first base. At that point, Foster surprised him by throwing a strike right across the plate.

The trick worked. Twice. Hartsel stood there and watched two straight strikes go by. Foster figured the gag would not fly a third time. So instead, he called out loudly to Hartsel. Foster accused him of illegally standing on the plate. Hartsel looked down at his feet just long enough for Foster to sneak strike three past him.

THE THINKING PLAYER BECOMES THINKING COACH

Foster's brilliant baseball mind was put to even greater use in 1907. That is when he became the manager of the Chicago Leland Giants. Today the hit-and-run is a standard baseball play. That is when a base runner takes off while the pitcher is throwing. The runner must trust that the batter will hit the ball in such a way that the runner will not get out. However, the hit-and-run was not a part of the game in the early part of the twentieth century. Not unless you played for Rube Foster, at least.

Indeed, Foster controlled the whole game from his bench. He told his pitchers what pitch to throw and where to throw it. He told his base runners whether or not to steal. He told his batters to take more pitches in order to tire the opposing pitcher's arm. Foster gave all these instructions in coded signals. Coaching signals are common today but were almost unheard of back then.

A NAP BECOMES A NIGHTMARE

As the president of the Negro National League, Rube Foster gained a reputation for being fair but ruthless. According to one story, Dayton Marcos owner John Matthews once took a nap during a league meeting. When Matthews awoke, Foster informed him that his team had been dismantled and the players on his roster had been split among the league's other teams.

Even today, however, nobody gives signs the way that Foster did. Foster was a pipe smoker. Many of his signals were related to this habit. During some games, Foster taking the

Rube Foster's half brother Bill Foster was considered to be one of the best left-handed pitchers in the Negro Leagues.

pipe out of his mouth meant the base runner should steal. In other games it might mean something different. Foster would sit there puffing on his pipe. Only his players knew what he was telling them to do next. In fact, even the puffs of smoke he exhaled could be a sign.

OWNING A TEAM, OWNING A LEAGUE

In 1911, Foster became owner of the Leland Giants. He quickly renamed them the Chicago American Giants. By coincidence, a local businessman named John Schorling had recently leased a baseball stadium. Schorling offered to join forces with Foster. With their own field to play on, the American Giants became one of the Negro Leagues' greatest teams.

But Foster was not content simply being the owner of one team. He wanted to oversee an entire league. And, starting in 1920, he did just that. In February of that year, seven owners got together in Kansas City, Missouri. They agreed to join together to form the NNL. It became black baseball's first successful professional league.

RUNS IN THE FAMILY

In 1918, Rube Foster's half brother Bill Foster tried out for a spot on his Chicago American Giants. Rube Foster cut his half brother. However, in 1923, the older Foster brought his younger half brother back. Bill Foster remained the Chicago American Giants' ace pitcher for much of the 1920s. In fact, many regard Bill Foster as the best left-handed pitcher in Negro Leagues history.

Bill Foster had many great achievements during his career.

Perhaps none is as famous as when he won both games of a doubleheader on a snowy day in 1926 to win the Negro World Series for his American Giants. After he shut down the Kansas City Monarchs in the first game, his teammates were asked who they wanted to pitch the next game. The reply was unanimous: "Foster!"

15

Rube Foster was known as "The Father of Black Baseball" for his impact as a player, team owner, and NNL president and secretary.

Foster was the one who had called this meeting. He immediately took control of the NNL as its president and secretary. The other owners let him do this because no one doubted that he was the right man, maybe even the only man, for the job.

Foster became ill in 1926 and had to resign his presidential post. People who cared about the NNL talked about him as though he had died. Writer Carl Beckwith wrote an article about Foster's resignation that sounded like an obituary. "The passing of Rube Foster from the baseball stage means the termination of the career of the best-known Negro baseball player in the entire world," Beckwith wrote.

Foster really did die in 1930. Thousands of people attended his wake and funeral. Those who could not fit in the church stood outside in the snow and waited to view his casket. Some stuck around for three days to pay their respects.

Many were not only mourning Foster's death but also the downfall of organized black baseball. In the four years since Foster's resignation, the NNL had sunk into financial trouble. Without him, some wondered if black baseball could survive.

Luckily, the answer was yes. In a few years, black leagues entered a new era and once again began to thrive. A new NNL was formed in 1933, and the Negro American League (NAL) followed in 1937. But no one who knew baseball's history would ever forget the debt that was owed to Andrew "Rube" Foster.

"SMOKEY JOE" WILLIAMS

Not too much is known about "Smokey Joe" Williams off the baseball field. Even his date and place of birth—April 6, 1886, in Seguin, Texas—is not certain. Unlike Andrew "Rube" Foster, whose funeral was attended by thousands, Williams died in obscurity. Even his year of death is disputed. Many believe he died in 1946. But historian John Holway claims Williams was still around in the early 1950s. The Baseball Hall of Fame lists his death as being in 1951. Such lack of certain knowledge about a black baseball star was common during the first half of the century.

Nobody can say for sure when Williams's life began and ended. But there is no doubt about his pitching abilities in between. Williams was one of the very best pitchers of his era. Some believe he was the best pitcher. Ty Cobb was the major leagues' greatest hitter at the beginning of the twentieth century. He once claimed that Williams would have been "a sure 30-game winner" if he had been allowed to pitch in the big leagues. Only the best MLB pitchers of the time could win 20 games in a season. It was especially rare for a pitcher to win 30.

Nobody can say for sure how many games Williams would have won in MLB. After all, he never had the opportunity to pitch in the majors. But there is evidence to back up Cobb's claim.

BABIES WITHOUT BIRTHDAYS

"Smokey Joe" Williams is not the only Negro Leaguer whose date of birth is difficult to pin down. That is because some states did not officially record black babies' births in the late nineteenth century. Among those states was Texas, where Williams was born. Without this documentation, baseball historians sometimes have to get creative to figure out approximate ages. Sometimes they talk to people who remember the ballplayer during his childhood. They can also check the US census records. Using sources such as those, the historians can then make an educated guess.

Williams compiled a 20–7 record during exhibition games he pitched against major league opponents. He twice outdueled Walter Johnson. Johnson is considered one of the greatest strikeout pitchers in MLB history. Indeed, one of Williams's first nicknames was "Strikeout."

It was during an encounter with Rube Foster that Williams earned another nickname. Williams was facing Foster's Chicago American Giants. After watching a couple of Williams's fastballs, Foster said, "Slow down there."

"Do you really want me to throw hard?" Williams asked. Then he reconsidered: "If I really throw hard, you won't see it at all."

Foster asked for the young pitcher's name. Williams replied, "Just call me Cyclone."

For a while, everyone did just that. Not much later, though, he received his most famous nickname. Williams was facing MLB's New York Giants in an exhibition game. He struck out 20 major league batters. Afterward, one of the Giants players patted Williams on the shoulder and said, "Nice job, Smokey." The name stuck for the rest of his career.

"Smokey Joe" Williams was known for his ability to strike out batters with his blazing fastball.

STRIKING EVERYBODY OUT

Williams was perhaps the most dominant pitcher of his or any other era. In 1912, he shut out the New York Giants. They had just played in the World Series. In 1915, he shut out the Philadelphia Phillies. The Phillies' pitcher that day was Hall of Famer Grover Cleveland Alexander. Alexander pitched well, giving up just one run. But Williams pitched better. His team won 1–0.

Williams was on the losing end of a 1–0 game against the New York Giants in 1917. Williams lost that game, but he certainly was not to blame. He struck out 20 batters that day. He did not give up a single hit, either. The Giants scored their only run because of a fielding error.

Williams had much success against the greatest black and white players of his era. However, his most famous game did not occur until August 7, 1930. Williams was approximately 45 years old by then. But he was still pitching astonishingly well. His age had slowed down his fastball, but not a whole lot. He could still get many batters to swing and miss. That was especially true during night games.

Seeing the ball at night can be difficult at times, even with modern lighting systems. On August 7, 1930, it was nearly impossible. Williams was pitching against Kansas City

Smokey Joe Williams warms up before a Homestead Grays game around 1928 in Pittsburgh.

Monarchs' ace Chet Brewer. At the time, Brewer was known for pitching cut balls. This meant he used an emery board, or a nail file, to scuff up the ball. A scratched baseball can move unpredictably through the air, making a batter's job that much harder. Cut balls were technically against the rules back then. Yet they were almost always tolerated. The combination of the poor lighting system and Brewer's nail file was lethal. Williams's team, the Homestead Grays, was helpless at the plate.

Williams had an answer for Brewer's nail file, though: pine tar. He rubbed the substance all over the ball. The pine tar made the ball sticky. It also turned the ball brown. Under poor lights, the ball was all but invisible to the Monarch standing in the batter's box.

The result of these two pitchers' trickery was 11 straight innings of scoreless baseball. Finally, in the 12th inning, the

CHET WAS NO CHEAT

Chet Brewer was known to cut the baseball with a nail file before hurling it toward the plate. Altering the ball like that is considered cheating in today's game. However, such trickery was often tolerated in the Negro Leagues. Besides, Brewer had several other excellent pitches in his arsenal. He also threw a sweeping curve, a sneaky sinker, and a screwball that curved in the opposite direction of his other pitches. His 24-year career was full of both All-Star games and travel. By the time he called it quits, he had pitched in Canada, Japan, the Philippines, Hawaii, Mexico, Panama, Puerto Rico, Haiti, and the Dominican Republic. Brewer never had an opportunity to pitch in the major leagues. But he did eventually pitch in the minor leagues in 1952. By then, however, he was in his mid-40s and had long since retired from black baseball. Brewer later served as a scout for the Pittsburgh Pirates.

Grays' Oscar Charleston walked. Then he scored on Chaney White's ground ball toward third base. The only reason White's ground ball ended the game was that it bounced off third base and none of the fielders could find where it landed. Charleston stepped safely onto home plate before they did. All in all, Brewer had struck out 19 batters, while "Smokey Joe" Williams had fanned 27.

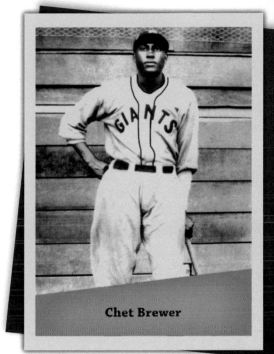

Chet Brewer

Williams went on to pitch for a couple more years. He then lived the rest of his life in Texas. The difficulty in pinning down a date of death suggests that most forgot about him as a person. But no one who ever saw Williams on the mound forgot about him as a player. In 1952 the *Pittsburgh Courier* polled former Negro Leaguers and asked them to pick the best Negro Leagues pitcher of all time. "Smokey Joe" Williams took first place in the poll, besting Leroy "Satchel" Paige by one vote.

3

WILBER "BULLET JOE" ROGAN

Wilber "Bullet Joe" Rogan was already 30 years old by the time he began pitching in the Negro Leagues. Yet he was already a baseball legend. Rogan had been in the armed forces from 1911 until 1919 and pitched on the army team. His overall record there was 50 wins and only 2 losses.

After leaving the service, Rogan joined the Kansas City Monarchs in 1920. Rogan had been born in Oklahoma in 1889. However, it was there, in the Kansas City area, where he spent most of his childhood.

Fans who had never seen the man before might not have believed in his past success. Rogan was only five-and-a-half feet tall. And he must have looked very tired. After all, he had been on a train for three days and nights in order to make his first pitching appearance.

If he had his skeptics, though, they soon became his admirers. That day Rogan pitched a one-hitter against Andrew "Rube" Foster's mighty Chicago American Giants. Then he continued to pitch just as well against every team he faced for the next decade. His lifetime Negro Leagues record was 116 wins and 50 losses.

ALL-AROUND EXCELLENCE

Wilber "Bullet Joe" Rogan played every position on the field, and he played each one well. As if that was not enough, Rogan also took a turn managing the Kansas City Monarchs. According to John "Buck" O'Neil, Rogan was a generous and knowledgeable coach who patiently taught players the finer points of hitting. After three decades of playing and managing, Rogan still had not had his fill of baseball. So he spent several more years as a Negro Leagues umpire. That gave him perhaps the most varied baseball resume of any man who ever played the game.

27

Wilber "Bullet Joe" Rogan, *front row*, *center*,
and the 1934 Kansas City Monarchs

Unlike most pitchers, Rogan was also a talented batter. The Monarchs had one of the best lineups at the time. Rogan hit right in the middle of it. Pitchers are usually stuck at the end of the batting order because they are the worst hitters. From 1922 to 1930, Rogan hit better than .300 every season. He hit equally well against white ball clubs, posting a .329 lifetime average. In 1924, he led the NNL in pitching wins and took second in batting average. During his prime, he won at least 20 games as a pitcher, hit well over .300, and belted more than 40 homers in a single season.

ROGAN V. THE SPITBALLER

Casey Stengel first competed against Bullet Joe Rogan during a game in Albuquerque, New Mexico. The man pitching for Stengel's team was a notorious spitballer. That meant he was known for spitting on the ball before throwing it to the plate. The spit would change the natural flight of the ball and make it harder to hit. Spitters were (and are) illegal, so Stengel did his best to avoid suspicion that his pitcher was cheating.

Stengel stood by home plate and offered a different explanation for the crazy way his pitcher's ball traveled through the air.

"Ladies and gentlemen," he'd say. "We're now going to have a young man that pitches this game today that throws the new, mysterious ball known as the 'tequila pitch'! It's taken from the tequila plant!"

The lie must have worked. Or at least no one cared that the pitcher was cheating. The pitcher continued to throw spitballs without anybody objecting, and Stengel's team won the game.

Rogan was no slouch in the field, either. Most Negro Leaguers considered him the best fielding pitcher in the game. Rogan was also an excellent outfielder. During one doubleheader, Rogan pitched and played four different positions.

Casey Stengel was both a player and a manager during his long, Hall of Fame career. He was from Kansas City, where Rogan ended up playing. When Stengel was a player, his team once faced off against Rogan's team. Although Stengel's barnstorming team won, he said Rogan was "one of the best, if not the best, pitcher that ever pitched."

Stengel was not the only one who felt that way. Baseball historian

AN EVEN LONGER TRIP

The three-day, three-night train ride Bullet Joe Rogan took to get to his first game with the Monarchs might seem like a long trip. However, it was nothing compared to the trips foreign players made to play ball in the United States. José Mendez of Cuba was one of the Negro Leagues' greatest pitchers during the early 1900s. There was one problem: he had dark skin. Many feel Mendez would have been invited to play in the major leagues if his skin had been lighter. New York Giants manager John McGraw claimed that Mendez was worth $50,000, a huge sum of money at the time. As it turned out, the major leagues' loss was the Negro Leagues' gain. In 1908, Mendez won 44 games and lost just two.

Phil Dixon believed that Rogan might very well be the greatest player who ever lived.

Rogan's son, also named Wilber, certainly agreed. "Satchel [Paige] needed a designated hitter when he was on the mound," he said. "When dad was on the mound, he was batting cleanup."

The Negro Leagues never actually used a designated hitter to replace the pitcher in the batting order, as the modern American League (AL) does. But Wilber "Bullet Joe" Rogan certainly did bat cleanup.

José Mendez

31

4

DICK "CANNONBALL" REDDING

There was never any confusion about why Dick Redding was called "Cannonball." Baseballs shot out of his arm as though they were from a cannon's blast. He threw so hard that professional athlete and scout Frank Forde swore he once saw a Redding fastball knock the bat right out of a swinging batter's hands. Redding once threw batting practice for the Detroit Tigers. However, the great hitter Ty Cobb refused to take any swings. Cobb was apparently afraid he would not be able to catch up to Redding's pitches.

Indeed, Cobb's fears were well founded. One time Redding faced off against baseball legend Babe Ruth's barnstorming team. Redding struck out Ruth three straight times in a total of nine pitches.

Redding's fastball was so fast that he did not need any other pitches for much of his career. Opponents knew they were going to get nothing but Redding's heater. Yet all they could do was whiff at it. Redding joined the Lincoln Giants in 1911. As a rookie, he won 17 consecutive games. In one game Redding struck out 25 batters in nine innings.

The next year, the great "Smokey Joe" Williams joined the Lincoln squad. That gave the Giants one of the best pitching duos in the history of professional baseball. By the end of the season, Redding had compiled a 43–12 record. In one game Redding struck out 25 batters in nine innings. Over the course of his career, he threw at least 30 no-hitters.

Dick "Cannonball" Redding

Redding was born in 1891 in Atlanta. He joined his first

Negro Leagues team, the Philadelphia Giants, as a 20-year-old. By then he looked the part of a menacing fastball pitcher. He stood 6-foot-4. His massive hands seemed to swallow up a baseball. Hall of Famer William "Judy" Johnson said those hands "looked like shovels."

Despite Redding's big body, he was in fact an easygoing guy. He rarely got fazed by much of anything. Like so many great athletes, he was able to shrug off failure and succeed the next time out. Still, there were times when his lack of concern got him in trouble.

QUIRKY CANNONBALL

Dick "Cannonball" Redding was a man with memorable quirks. Like many ballplayers, he was superstitious. If he was on a winning streak, he would not change or wash his undershirt until it became stiff with sweat. Even then the shirt did not get cleaned until one of his teammates could no longer stand the odor. Once, Redding washed his shirt and then promptly lost a game. He reported that the now-soft fabric had left him feeling weak on the mound. If he was not holding his clothing responsible for a loss, he might have blamed his glove. Redding often replaced his "faulty" gloves.

Cannonball Redding, *right*, had a fastball so fast that contemporaries compared his arm to a cannon.

FLAT TIRE

Once, on a road trip, one of Redding's team's cars had a flat tire. Redding was with some other teammates in another car. They had to turn around and drive 20 miles (32.2 km) to purchase a spare tire. Once they retrieved the spare, it was Redding's job to hold the tire on the car's running board as they drove to find the rest of their team.

"Okay, Dick," one of his teammates said once they arrived back at the car, "give me that tire."

"Huh?" Redding replied.

It was the middle of the night, and Redding had dozed off. He had also managed to let go

NOT SO EASYGOING

Another great Negro Leagues pitcher was Leon Day. Unlike Cannonball Redding, Day was not known for his easygoing nature. If he thought a batter was standing too comfortably at the plate, he did not hesitate to throw his fastball high and inside. In fact, he did that even if the batter only had one arm.

While pitching in Ocean City, Maryland, Day gave up a hit to the one-armed Pete Gray. He said to Gray, "Wait till you come back up the next time." Sure enough, Day got his revenge during Gray's next at-bat. Gray had barely stepped into the batter's box before having to jump out of it. Day had sent a fastball toward his neck, and Gray was unable to get a hit in that at-bat—or any others that day.

Right-hander Leon Day was known as one of the greatest Negro Leagues pitchers during the late 1930s and 1940s. However, he was also known for his temper.

of the tire. It went rolling across the road somewhere over the 20-mile span they had just driven. It was too dark to go looking for it. Instead, they had to turn around again and buy

HESITATION PITCH

As Cannonball Redding got older, his fastball slowed down at least a few miles per hour. So he developed other pitches, including a hesitation pitch. Leroy "Satchel" Paige would later become famous for his hesitation pitches. Yet Redding was the first to try such a thing. In mid-windup he would twist so that the batter could see the number on the back of his jersey. He would stay like that, balancing on one leg, for several seconds. Then Redding would suddenly unwind and deliver one of his vicious fastballs.

another tire. At the time, his teammates were in no laughing mood. However, the incident became a fond memory.

A CAREER WINDING DOWN

Redding was at his prime during the 1910s. That was also the time when World War I was raging in Europe. Although Redding was not allowed to play in MLB, he did serve for the US armed forces in 1918 and 1919. His professional playing career did not last long after that. But after a stint as a player-manager, Redding served as a manager for many years after that.

Dick "Cannonball" Redding was one of a kind. Although his happy-go-lucky personality sometimes got him in trouble, it was usually appreciated. Later, as a manager, his players enjoyed the freedom he gave them to play the way that suited their games. Ted Page was one of the fastest men on Redding's team. Redding let Page try to steal a base whenever he felt he could make it.

Of course, Redding's legacy will always have more to do with his pitching than anything else. And few in baseball history could boast a fastball like his.

GIANTS EVERYWHERE

When reading about the Negro Leagues, it can seem as if every team was named the Giants. There were the Bacharach Giants, the Lincoln Giants, the Brooklyn Giants, the Brooklyn Royal Giants, the Brooklyn Cuban Giants, and many, many more. According to Negro Leagues legend John "Buck" O'Neil, the reason for this was that *Giants* was a code word. In many white communities, newspapers refused to print pictures of black ballplayers. But that did not mean the people in the community did not want to watch black ball clubs. If anything, the black teams often played a more exciting brand of baseball than the white teams. If fans saw that the Giants were coming to town, they could assume it was a black team and know they were going to get their money's worth.

5

LEROY "SATCHEL" PAIGE

Of all the extraordinary pitchers in the Negro Leagues, the greatest of them all was unquestionably Leroy "Satchel" Paige. That is not to say he was the best. Baseball historians and former players have made strong arguments for several other Negro Leagues pitchers as being the best. But no other pitcher—or player, for that matter— combined so much talent with so much showmanship. Fans came in droves to watch Paige play.

Paige's feats on the diamond are legendary. People say he threw his fastball so hard that it made a buzzing sound as it moved through the air. That is why he called it his bee ball. If it did make a sound, batters were likely grateful. After all, it was the only way they could track the pitch. The ball moved so swiftly, some say, that the naked eye could barely catch a glimpse of it. One time, it has been claimed, Paige's bee ball vanished altogether. The umpire had to stop the game to look for it.

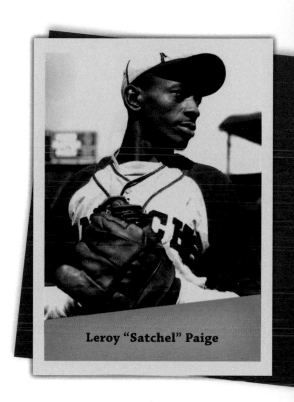

Leroy "Satchel" Paige

The truth of these legends is beside the point. What matters is that behind them was a very real, amazing man with a very real, amazing life story.

SATCHEL TREE

Many believe Paige was born in 1906 in Mobile, Alabama. However, nobody knows for sure, and Paige was often coy about his age. He grew up poor. In fact, his family was so poor that he had to get a job when he was only seven years old. Paige became a porter for the railroad station. That meant he toted people's luggage to and from their trains.

PERFECT AIM

Like many things about Leroy "Satchel" Paige, his pinpoint control was legendary. At his first professional tryout, Paige was asked to stand 60 feet away from a fence. Fifteen cans were set on top of this fence. Paige was given the same number of pitches to knock them off. In the end, only one can was left standing. To entertain fans, Paige was known to put a bucket on top of home plate and a baseball on top of the bucket. From the mound he would bet people he could knock the ball off the bucket in no more than three tries. It was a bet he rarely lost.

Each bag Paige carried earned him a nickel or a dime. However, Paige was so small that he could only pick up one bag at a time. So he came up with an idea to help increase his income. Paige made a sling out of poles and ropes that allowed him to carry several bags at once. The device was creative. But other porters thought it made him look ridiculous. They told him he looked like a "satchel tree."

The name stuck. Years later, after he had become a baseball celebrity, even the newspapers referred to him by his nickname. Box scores would list all of his teammates' last names. But for Paige, they would list him simply as Satchel.

Growing up, Paige might have thought the only reason his name would make the paper was because he had gotten into trouble. He was only 12 when he was caught stealing toy rings. Paige was then sent to a reform school in Mt. Meigs, Alabama. This punishment ended up being a blessing. It was in reform school that Paige was forced to get an education. He had never liked school before and often skipped class. It was also in reform school that Paige learned to pitch.

THE LEGENDS ARE BORN

Paige was at Mt. Meigs for five years. By the time he was finished at the reform school, he was 6-foot-4. However, Paige was lanky at only 140 pounds. Being skinny was not just a phase, either. Though he put on some weight as he grew older, Paige had the same gangly limbs for the rest of his life.

One of these gangly limbs was his right arm. It could propel a baseball faster than many had ever seen. Paige threw the ball so hard that it seemed to hop just before it reached the plate. Just as importantly, it seemed to go exactly where he aimed. His incredible control made him almost unhittable. Many hitters were grateful for that. After all, it was better to go hitless than to get hit by one of Paige's fastballs.

STRONG ARM, STRONGER PERSONALITY

It did not take teams long to realize how good Paige was. In just a few years, he was one of the most sought-after pitchers in black baseball. In 1924, while playing for the Mobile Tigers, he made $1 a game if he was lucky. Some days he was paid in lemonade. Two years later, the Chattanooga Black Lookouts offered him $50 a month. Two years after that, the Birmingham Black Barons upped his monthly contract to $275. However, that was still considerably less than what MLB stars were making. For example, Philadelphia Athletics' star pitcher Lefty Grove earned more than $20,000 per season during the late 1920s and early 1930s.

There was something else these teams learned quickly: Paige played baseball on his own terms or not at all. Often, his demands were good for black baseball. At the time, many towns would not allow a black man to sleep in a hotel or eat in a restaurant. Paige refused to pitch in those towns. If fans wanted to see him pitch, they needed to provide food and shelter to him and his teammates.

Hall of Famer Grover Cleveland Alexander watches Satchel Paige warm up ahead of a 1941 game at Yankee Stadium. Paige was pitching for the New York Black Yankees.

He also took stands against racism from the mound. One time, Paige's pitches were unusually wild during a game against a white semiprofessional team in Denver. He walked two batters in a row. Then he gave up an infield single to load the bases. One of the players from the opposing dugout called Paige a derogatory term. Then the player claimed that Paige was overrated.

Paige turned to his first baseman, John "Buck" O'Neil. He told O'Neil to bring the outfielders in. So O'Neil signaled for the outfielders to take a few steps closer to the infield. Paige was not satisfied. "Bring them *in*," he repeated. O'Neil waved them a few steps closer. But once again Paige objected. He told O'Neil to bring them *all the way* in. Paige continued to wait

BETTER LATE THAN NEVER

One time Satchel Paige showed up in the middle of the third inning with a runner on first base. Because he was Satchel Paige—and the fans had paid good money to see him pitch—he was inserted into the game the second he arrived at the stadium. This meant that Paige had not yet had a chance to warm up. But he had a solution to this problem. Instead of throwing home, Paige kept trying to "pick off" the base runner at first. Of course, what he was actually doing was playing a leisurely game of catch with the first baseman. When his arm finally felt loose enough to pitch to the plate, he was nearly unhittable. The other team was unable to score a single run for the remainder of the game.

until all seven teammates—the outfielders and the infielders—were kneeling by the mound. Then he struck out the next three batters on nine straight pitches. The crowd applauded enthusiastically and the Denver players apologized for their teammate's remark.

NOT ALWAYS POSITIVE

Other times, Paige's refusal to do things any way but his own was more puzzling for his teammates. He had a habit of arriving late to games. Sometimes his lateness was the result of getting pulled over by police. Paige received many speeding tickets. Other times he skipped the first few innings in order to go fishing. When he would finally make it to the game, he would give the umpire a fish.

These sorts of incidents were amusing nuisances to the team. However, they were tolerable so long as Paige eventually arrived to save the day. Unfortunately, though, he often failed to show up at all. He had a history of quitting teams even after agreeing to contracts with them. By 1931, he had jumped from the Mobile Tigers to the Chattanooga Black Lookouts to the Birmingham Black Barons to the Black Sox of Baltimore to the Nashville Elite Giants to the Cleveland Cubs to the Pittsburgh Crawfords. As Negro Leaguers legend and Paige teammate

Satchel Paige, *back row second from left,* **played for the famous Pittsburgh Crawfords in 1932.**

James "Cool Papa" Bell said, "If you showed him money or a car, you could lead him anywhere."

In 1936, Paige was in his second stint with the Pittsburgh Crawfords. They were one of the most famous Negro League teams ever. However, Paige abandoned the team again.

This time Paige went to play in the Dominican Republic. That country had a dictator named Rafael Trujillo. He was trying to put together the best baseball team in the world. Trujillo wanted Paige to be his ace pitcher.

Baseball played a very important role in that country's politics. A man who fielded a great team was challenging Trujillo's dictatorship. Trujillo believed an even better team could help him prove beyond any doubt that he held absolute power over his country.

The reason Paige agreed to play for the team was simple: money. Trujillo offered him $30,000 to play for Trujillo's Dragones in 1937. That amount of money was unheard of at the time in the Negro Leagues. And Trujillo said he would pay the same amount to any teammates who joined Paige.

William "Gus" Greenlee was the owner of the Crawfords. He was also president of the NAL. Greenlee was furious when he heard he had lost Paige and several more of his players. So Greenlee banned each of them for life.

Sure enough, Trujillo's team did win his country's championship series. His US players returned home with stories of armed guards watching their every move. In the end, the Negro Leagues reduced their punishment to a small fine. For better or worse, the Negro Leagues could not afford to kick out its best players. That was especially true of Paige. He was by now the most famous player in the history of black baseball.

SATCHEL'S SORE ARM

Paige later left his Negro Leagues contract yet again and went to play for a team in Mexico. While there, he developed a sore arm. Paige blamed the spicy food. He said it had disturbed his delicate stomach and then spread poisonously to his right arm. The soreness was most likely caused by overuse, however. Today, starting pitchers usually start one of every five games. And the best pitchers only pitch a handful of complete games each year. That was not the case during Paige's era. Once he pitched every day for a month. The result of so many innings pitched was that Paige was no longer able to throw his bee ball.

All of a sudden, no teams wanted anything to do with Paige. For years they had put up with his antics. That was because his right arm could almost always guarantee fans for their ballclub. But now his right arm was not working so well, and no one had any use for him.

Satchel Paige shows off his famous high leg kick before a 1942 game. He was pitching for the New York Black Yankees at the time.

MORE THAN SATCHEL'S SIDEKICK

Toward the end of his life, Hilton Smith was reportedly bitter about being portrayed as Satchel Paige's sidekick. To some extent, this label was unavoidable. Anyone who pitched with Paige was pitching in his tremendous shadow. In many games, Paige would pitch the first three innings, then Smith would relieve him. When people asked why Paige's arm looked so straight and Smith's so crooked, Smith would say, "Satchel pitched three. I pitched six!" Still, while future generations of baseball fans may have overlooked Smith's contributions, his fellow players did not. Many who played with and against Smith considered his curveball to be the best in baseball.

No one, that is, except J. L. Wilkinson. Wilkinson owned the Kansas City Monarchs, another one of the most famous Negro Leagues teams. Wilkinson knew Paige was in no condition to pitch for the Monarchs. But he also knew Paige's fame could sell tickets. So Wilkinson put Paige on his Little Monarchs team and renamed them the Satchel Paige All-Stars. It was really more like a minor league squad. Yet this team often got more press than the *real* Monarchs.

Then, one day in 1941, Paige's arm came back to life. He could still not throw the ball quite as hard as he had earlier in his career. But he could once again throw it harder than most. And he had added more pitches that included a curveball and a hesitation pitch. If anything, some say he became a better pitcher than he had been in his flame-throwing youth.

SATCHEL FINALLY SETTLES IN

For the next several years, Paige finally stuck with one team: the Kansas City Monarchs. It was as a Monarch that Paige put into motion the most talked about sequence of events in Negro Leagues history.

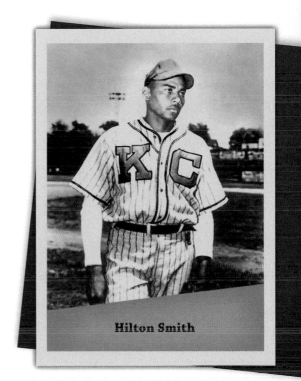

Hilton Smith

The Monarchs were playing the Homestead Grays in the 1942 Negro World Series. Pitcher Hilton Smith had started the game for the Monarchs and had pitched well. In more than five innings he had not given up a single run. Still, Paige came in to relieve his teammate. In the seventh, Paige gave up a triple. According to legend, that was when he turned once again to his first baseman, Buck O'Neil.

He called O'Neil over and laid out his plan. Paige was going to intentionally walk the next two batters. That would load the bases and allow him to pitch to Josh Gibson. He was one of the best hitters in black baseball and quite possibly the world.

John "Buck" O'Neil

O'Neil thought Paige had lost his mind. O'Neil called for their manager, Frank Duncan. When Duncan heard Paige's plan, all he could do was walk wearily back to the dugout. He might have been the manager, but he knew who was in control. Once Paige got a notion in his head, there was no talking him out of it.

So Paige walked the men in front of Gibson. As he did, he held a conversation with the great hitter. He told him that this at-bat would prove once and for all who was the better player. Gibson was not disturbed by this taunting. He approached the plate and dug into the batter's box.

Paige reared back and hurled a fastball by Gibson. Before throwing the next pitch, Paige announced he was throwing another fastball. Gibson must not have believed him, because once again he did not swing at a strike. For the last pitch, Paige gave Gibson a side-armed curveball. Strike three. Legend says the mighty Gibson had struck out without ever lifting the bat off his shoulder.

HONORING THEIR PAST

Once, Satchel Paige and Buck O'Neil visited Drum Island in South Carolina. In that spot during the mid-1800s, black slaves had been auctioned off to the highest bidder. For a long time, Paige and O'Neil stood together silently and stared at a tree with a plaque on it. The slave market had been right there. After a while Paige said, "Seems like I've been here before." O'Neil agreed, and the two men continued to look at the tree and to see their ancestors.

CROSSING THE COLOR LINE

In 1947, Jackie Robinson played his first game for the Brooklyn Dodgers. That signaled the beginning of the end of MLB's color line. Other MLB teams slowly but surely began signing black players after that.

On July 9, 1948, at age 42, Paige became the first black pitcher in the AL. He pitched two scoreless innings in relief for the Cleveland Indians. Paige went on to help the Indians win the World Series.

Paige was already in his 40s by this point. Yet he continued to pitch. He pitched in the majors, the minors, in the Negro Leagues, and on touring teams for two more decades. His last stint in the big leagues was with the Kansas City Athletics in 1965. Paige was 59 years old. That day he threw three more scoreless innings. He also set a record as the oldest player in MLB history.

Still, Paige's days in the majors took place well past his prime. Though his arm remained tireless, it was not as explosive as it had been. All of his greatest years had been spent in the Negro Leagues. Fans and historians could only listen to the stories and imagine how good he would have been had he been able to play his entire career in the major leagues.

Many regard Satchel Paige to be the greatest player in Negro Leagues history.

TIMELINE

1859

The Henson Base Ball Club faces the Weeksville Unknowns in the first known baseball game between all-black teams.

1900

No black players are left in Major League Baseball.

1920

The first Negro National League is formed.

1922: PITCHERS' DUEL

One of the great pitchers' duels of all time took place on September 16. Chicago beat Atlantic City 1–0 in 20 innings. Harold Treadwell pitched all 20 innings for Atlantic City. For Chicago, Huck Rile pitched six innings. Dave Brown, who had pitched nine innings two days earlier, came on in relief and pitched the final 14 innings without allowing a run.

1932: "DOUBLE DUTY" RADCLIFFE

Ted "Double Duty" Radcliffe of the Pittsburgh Crawfords earned his nickname with an impressive feat. In a doubleheader in 1932, Radcliffe caught a shutout by Satchel Paige in the first game, and then pitched a shutout of his own in the second game.

1933

The second Negro National League is formed.

1937: TRUJILLO'S DRAGONES

When Satchel Paige accepted an offer to play for Trujillo's Dragones in 1937—the team run by Dominican Republic dictator Rafael Trujillo—he brought some of the Negro Leagues' best players with him. Among them were hitters James "Cool Papa" Bell, Josh Gibson, and Sam Bankhead as well as pitcher Leroy Matlock. Not surprisingly, the Dragones won the league title.

1937

The Negro American League is formed.

1941

Negro Leagues popularity soars while the United States fights in World War II.

1947

Jackie Robinson plays for the Brooklyn Dodgers.

1965: OLDEST ROOKIE

Satchel Paige's prime years came during his time in the Negro Leagues. He continued pitching long after that, though. In 1965, the Kansas City Athletics brought Paige out of retirement. He pitched three innings for the A's and thus became the oldest person to play in MLB, at age 59.

1971

Leroy "Satchel" Paige is inducted into the National Baseball Hall of Fame.

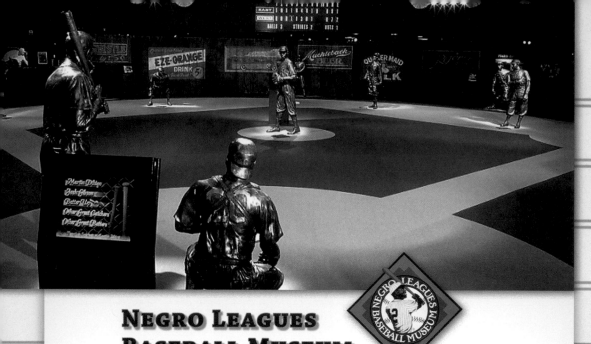

NEGRO LEAGUES BASEBALL MUSEUM

1616 East 18th Street
Kansas City, MO 64108-1610
816-221-1920
www.nlbm.com

The Negro Leagues Baseball Museum preserves the history of Negro Leagues baseball through interactive exhibits, films, photos, sculptures, and artifacts. The museum does not serve as a hall of fame for black baseball. Because the sport is no longer segregated, the Negro Leagues Baseball Museum recognizes the National Baseball Hall of Fame in Cooperstown, New York, as the shrine for all of baseball's greatest players.

The museum opened in 1994 and moved into a new 10,000-square-foot space in 1997. It is located in the historic 18th & Vine Jazz District, a traditional center for black culture in Kansas City. The Paseo YMCA building, where the Negro National League was founded in 1920, is nearby.

GLOSSARY

ace
A team's best starting pitcher.

barnstorming
When a team travels around and faces various opponents rather than playing in a traditional league.

color line
An unwritten rule within MLB that prevented black players from playing in the majors until Jackie Robinson joined the Brooklyn Dodgers in 1947.

commissioner
The person in charge of baseball's major and minor leagues.

contracts
Binding agreements about, for example, years of commitment by a baseball player in exchange for a given salary.

derogatory
Something that is negative toward something else.

discrimination
Treating people differently based on prejudice.

doubleheader
A set of two baseball games played between the same two teams on the same day.

exhibition
A game in which the teams play to develop skills and promote the sport rather than for a competitive advantage.

scout
A person who watches baseball games to help prepare for upcoming games or to identify talented players for a team to add.

segregated
When groups of people were legally separated from each other.

semiprofessional
A level below professional in which players are paid but not enough to survive on as a full-time job.

FOR MORE INFORMATION

Select Bibliography

Dixon, Phil. *The Monarchs 1920–1938: Featuring Wilber "Bullet" Rogan, the Greatest Ballplayer in Cooperstown*. Sioux Falls, SD: Mariah Press, 2002.

Hogan, Lawrence D. *Shades of Glory*. Washington DC: National Geographic Society, 2006.

Holway, John. *The Complete Book of the Negro Leagues: The Other Half of Baseball History*. Fern Park, FL: Hastings House Publishers, 2001.

O'Neil, Buck. *I Was Right on Time*. New York: Simon & Schuster, 1996.

Peterson, Robert. *Only the Ball Was White*. New York: Oxford University Press, 1970.

Further Readings

Nelson, Kadir. *We Are the Ship: The Story of Negro League Baseball*. New York: Jump at the Sun/Hyperion Books for Children, 2008.

Smith, Charles R. *Stars in the Shadows: The Negro League All-Star Game of 1934*. New York: Atheneum, 2012.

Sturm, James, and Rich Tommaso. *Satchel Paige: Striking Out Jim Crow*. New York: Jump at the Sun, 2007.

Weatherford, Carole Boston. *A Negro League Scrapbook*. Honesdale, PA: Boyds Mills Press, 2005.

Withers, Ernest C. *Negro League Baseball*. New York: Harry N. Abrams, 2004.

Web Links

To learn more about the Negro Leagues, visit ABDO Publishing Company online at **www.abdopublishing.com**. Web sites about the Negro Leagues are featured on our Book Links page. These links are routinely monitored and updated to provide the most current information available.

Places to Visit

Highmark Legacy Square

PNC Park
115 Federal Street
Pittsburgh, PA 15212
412-325-4700
http://pittsburgh.pirates.mlb.com/pit/community/legacysquare.jsp
Located just outside the Pittsburgh Pirates' PNC Park, Highmark Legacy Square offers interactive exhibits dedicated to preserving the history of the Negro Leagues, including the local Homestead Grays and Pittsburgh Crawfords.

National Baseball Hall of Fame

25 Main Street
Cooperstown, NY 13326
888-HALL-OF-FAME
www.baseballhall.org
This hall of fame and museum highlights the greatest players and moments in the history of baseball. Over the last several decades, several former Negro Leaguers have been inducted and enshrined here.

INDEX

About the Author: Paul Hoblin has written several sports books. He has an MFA from the University of Minnesota.